ESV

ILLUMINATED
SCRIPTURE JOURNAL

ENGLISH STANDARD VERSION

JAMES

CROSSWAY

WHEATON, ILLINOIS — ESV.ORG

RRDS	27	26	25	24	23	22
18	17	16	15	14		

PREFACE

The Bible

The words of the Bible are the very words of God our Creator speaking to us. They are completely truthful;[1] they are pure;[2] they are powerful;[3] and they are wise and righteous.[4] We should read these words with reverence and awe,[5] and with joy and delight.[6] Through these words God gives us eternal life,[7] and daily nourishes our spiritual lives.[8]

The ESV Translation

The English Standard Version® (ESV®) stands in the classic stream of English Bible translations that goes back nearly five centuries. In this stream, accurate faithfulness to the original text is combined with simplicity, beauty, and dignity of expression. Our goal has been to carry forward this legacy for this generation and generations to come.

The ESV is an "essentially literal" translation that seeks as far as possible to reproduce the meaning and structure of the original text and the personal style of each Bible writer. We have sought to be "as literal as possible" while maintaining clear expression and literary excellence. Therefore the ESV is well suited for both personal reading and church ministry, for devotional reflection and serious study, and for Scripture memorization.

---

[1] Ps. 119:160; Prov. 30:5; Titus 1:2; Heb. 6:18 [2] Ps. 12:6 [3] Jer. 23:29; Heb. 4:12; 1 Pet. 1:23 [4] Ps. 19:7–11 [5] Deut. 28:58; Ps. 119:74; Isa. 66:2 [6] Ps. 19:7–11; 119:14, 97, 103; Jer. 15:16 [7] John 6:68; 1 Pet. 1:23 [8] Deut. 32:46; Matt. 4:4

The ESV Publishing Team

The ESV publishing team has included more than a hundred people. The fourteen-member Translation Oversight Committee benefited from the work of fifty biblical experts serving as Translation Review Scholars and from the comments of the more than fifty members of the Advisory Council. This international team from many denominations shares a common commitment to the truth of God's Word and to historic Christian orthodoxy.

To God's Honor and Praise

We know that no Bible translation is perfect; but we also know that God uses imperfect and inadequate things to his honor and praise. So to God the Father, Son, and Holy Spirit— and to his people—we offer what we have done, with our prayers that it may prove useful, with gratitude for much help given, and with ongoing wonder that our God should ever have entrusted to us so momentous a task.

To God alone be the glory!
The Translation Oversight Committee

JAMES

Greeting

1 James, a servant of God and of the Lord Jesus Christ,
To the twelve tribes in the Dispersion:
Greetings.

Testing of Your Faith

²Count it all joy, my brothers, when you meet trials of various kinds, ³for you know that the testing of your faith produces steadfastness. ⁴And let steadfastness have its full effect, that you may be perfect and complete, lacking in nothing.

⁵If any of you lacks wisdom, let him ask God, who gives generously to all without reproach, and it will be given him. ⁶But let him ask in faith, with no doubting, for the one who doubts is like a wave of the sea that is driven and tossed by the wind. ⁷For that person must not suppose that he will receive anything from the Lord; ⁸he is a double-minded man, unstable in all his ways.

⁹Let the lowly brother boast in his exaltation, ¹⁰and the rich in his humiliation, because like a flower of the grass he will pass away. ¹¹For the sun rises with its scorching heat and withers the grass; its flower falls, and its beauty perishes. So also will the rich man fade away in the midst of his pursuits.

¹²Blessed is the man who remains steadfast under trial, for when he has stood the test he will receive the crown of life,

which God has promised to those who love him. [13] Let no one say when he is tempted, "I am being tempted by God," for God cannot be tempted with evil, and he himself tempts no one. [14] But each person is tempted when he is lured and enticed by his own desire. [15] Then desire when it has conceived gives birth to sin, and sin when it is fully grown brings forth death.

[16] Do not be deceived, my beloved brothers. [17] Every good gift and every perfect gift is from above, coming down from the Father of lights, with whom there is no variation or shadow due to change. [18] Of his own will he brought us forth by the word of truth, that we should be a kind of firstfruits of his creatures.

Hearing and Doing the Word

[19] Know this, my beloved brothers: let every person be quick to hear, slow to speak, slow to anger; [20] for the anger of man does not produce the righteousness of God. [21] Therefore put away all filthiness and rampant wickedness and receive with meekness the implanted word, which is able to save your souls.

[22] But be doers of the word, and not hearers only, deceiving yourselves. [23] For if anyone is a hearer of the word and not a doer, he is like a man who looks intently at his natural face in a mirror. [24] For he looks at himself and goes away and at once forgets what he was like. [25] But the one who looks into the perfect law, the law of liberty, and perseveres, being no hearer who forgets but a doer who acts, he will be blessed in his doing.

[26] If anyone thinks he is religious and does not bridle his tongue but deceives his heart, this person's religion is worthless. [27] Religion that is pure and undefiled before God the

BUT BE
DOERS
OF THE
WORD
AND NOT
HEARERS ONLY
JAMES 1:22

Father is this: to visit orphans and widows in their affliction, and to keep oneself unstained from the world.

The Sin of Partiality

2 My brothers, show no partiality as you hold the faith in our Lord Jesus Christ, the Lord of glory. [2] For if a man wearing a gold ring and fine clothing comes into your assembly, and a poor man in shabby clothing also comes in, [3] and if you pay attention to the one who wears the fine clothing and say, "You sit here in a good place," while you say to the poor man, "You stand over there," or, "Sit down at my feet," [4] have you not then made distinctions among yourselves and become judges with evil thoughts? [5] Listen, my beloved brothers, has not God chosen those who are poor in the world to be rich in faith and heirs of the kingdom, which he has promised to those who love him? [6] But you have dishonored the poor man. Are not the rich the ones who oppress you, and the ones who drag you into court? [7] Are they not the ones who blaspheme the honorable name by which you were called?

[8] If you really fulfill the royal law according to the Scripture, "You shall love your neighbor as yourself," you are doing well. [9] But if you show partiality, you are committing sin and are convicted by the law as transgressors. [10] For whoever keeps the whole law but fails in one point has become guilty of all of it. [11] For he who said, "Do not commit adultery," also said, "Do not murder." If you do not commit adultery but do murder, you have become a transgressor of the law. [12] So speak and so act as those who are to be judged under the law of liberty. [13] For judgment is without mercy to one who has shown no mercy. Mercy triumphs over judgment.

Faith Without Works Is Dead

¹⁴ What good is it, my brothers, if someone says he has faith but does not have works? Can that faith save him? ¹⁵ If a brother or sister is poorly clothed and lacking in daily food, ¹⁶ and one of you says to them, "Go in peace, be warmed and filled," without giving them the things needed for the body, what good is that? ¹⁷ So also faith by itself, if it does not have works, is dead.

¹⁸ But someone will say, "You have faith and I have works." Show me your faith apart from your works, and I will show you my faith by my works. ¹⁹ You believe that God is one; you do well. Even the demons believe—and shudder! ²⁰ Do you want to be shown, you foolish person, that faith apart from works is useless? ²¹ Was not Abraham our father justified by works when he offered up his son Isaac on the altar? ²² You see that faith was active along with his works, and faith was completed by his works; ²³ and the Scripture was fulfilled that says, "Abraham believed God, and it was counted to him as righteousness"— and he was called a friend of God. ²⁴ You see that a person is justified by works and not by faith alone. ²⁵ And in the same way was not also Rahab the prostitute justified by works when she received the messengers and sent them out by another way? ²⁶ For as the body apart from the spirit is dead, so also faith apart from works is dead.

Taming the Tongue

3 Not many of you should become teachers, my brothers, for you know that we who teach will be judged with greater strictness. ² For we all stumble in many ways. And if anyone does not stumble in what he says, he is a perfect man, able also to bridle his whole body. ³ If we put bits into the mouths of

SO ALSO

Faith

BY ITSELF,

IF IT DOES NOT HAVE

WORKS,

IS DEAD.

JAMES 2:17

horses so that they obey us, we guide their whole bodies as well.
⁴ Look at the ships also: though they are so large and are driven
by strong winds, they are guided by a very small rudder wher-
ever the will of the pilot directs. ⁵ So also the tongue is a small
member, yet it boasts of great things.

How great a forest is set ablaze by such a small fire! ⁶ And the
tongue is a fire, a world of unrighteousness. The tongue is set
among our members, staining the whole body, setting on fire
the entire course of life, and set on fire by hell. ⁷ For every kind
of beast and bird, of reptile and sea creature, can be tamed and
has been tamed by mankind, ⁸ but no human being can tame the
tongue. It is a restless evil, full of deadly poison. ⁹ With it we bless
our Lord and Father, and with it we curse people who are made in
the likeness of God. ¹⁰ From the same mouth come blessing and
cursing. My brothers, these things ought not to be so. ¹¹ Does
a spring pour forth from the same opening both fresh and salt
water? ¹² Can a fig tree, my brothers, bear olives, or a grapevine
produce figs? Neither can a salt pond yield fresh water.

Wisdom from Above

¹³ Who is wise and understanding among you? By his good
conduct let him show his works in the meekness of wisdom.
¹⁴ But if you have bitter jealousy and selfish ambition in your
hearts, do not boast and be false to the truth. ¹⁵ This is not the
wisdom that comes down from above, but is earthly, unspiri-
tual, demonic. ¹⁶ For where jealousy and selfish ambition exist,
there will be disorder and every vile practice. ¹⁷ But the wisdom
from above is first pure, then peaceable, gentle, open to reason,
full of mercy and good fruits, impartial and sincere. ¹⁸ And a har-
vest of righteousness is sown in peace by those who make peace.

Warning Against Worldliness

4 What causes quarrels and what causes fights among you? Is it not this, that your passions are at war within you? ² You desire and do not have, so you murder. You covet and cannot obtain, so you fight and quarrel. You do not have, because you do not ask. ³ You ask and do not receive, because you ask wrongly, to spend it on your passions. ⁴ You adulterous people! Do you not know that friendship with the world is enmity with God? Therefore whoever wishes to be a friend of the world makes himself an enemy of God. ⁵ Or do you suppose it is to no purpose that the Scripture says, "He yearns jealously over the spirit that he has made to dwell in us"? ⁶ But he gives more grace. Therefore it says, "God opposes the proud but gives grace to the humble." ⁷ Submit yourselves therefore to God. Resist the devil, and he will flee from you. ⁸ Draw near to God, and he will draw near to you. Cleanse your hands, you sinners, and purify your hearts, you double-minded. ⁹ Be wretched and mourn and weep. Let your laughter be turned to mourning and your joy to gloom. ¹⁰ Humble yourselves before the Lord, and he will exalt you.

¹¹ Do not speak evil against one another, brothers. The one who speaks against a brother or judges his brother, speaks evil against the law and judges the law. But if you judge the law, you are not a doer of the law but a judge. ¹² There is only one lawgiver and judge, he who is able to save and to destroy. But who are you to judge your neighbor?

Boasting About Tomorrow

¹³ Come now, you who say, "Today or tomorrow we will go into such and such a town and spend a year there and trade and

SUBMIT

YOURSELVES THEREFORE TO

GOD

RESIST THE DEVIL

&

HE WILL FLEE FROM

YOU.

JAMES 4:7

make a profit"— [14] yet you do not know what tomorrow will bring. What is your life? For you are a mist that appears for a little time and then vanishes. [15] Instead you ought to say, "If the Lord wills, we will live and do this or that." [16] As it is, you boast in your arrogance. All such boasting is evil. [17] So whoever knows the right thing to do and fails to do it, for him it is sin.

Warning to the Rich

5 Come now, you rich, weep and howl for the miseries that are coming upon you. [2] Your riches have rotted and your garments are moth-eaten. [3] Your gold and silver have corroded, and their corrosion will be evidence against you and will eat your flesh like fire. You have laid up treasure in the last days. [4] Behold, the wages of the laborers who mowed your fields, which you kept back by fraud, are crying out against you, and the cries of the harvesters have reached the ears of the Lord of hosts. [5] You have lived on the earth in luxury and in self-indulgence. You have fattened your hearts in a day of slaughter. [6] You have condemned and murdered the righteous person. He does not resist you.

Patience in Suffering

[7] Be patient, therefore, brothers, until the coming of the Lord. See how the farmer waits for the precious fruit of the earth, being patient about it, until it receives the early and the late rains. [8] You also, be patient. Establish your hearts, for the coming of the Lord is at hand. [9] Do not grumble against one another, brothers, so that you may not be judged; behold, the Judge is standing at the door. [10] As an example of suffering and patience, brothers, take the prophets who spoke in the

name of the Lord. ¹¹ Behold, we consider those blessed who
remained steadfast. You have heard of the steadfastness of
Job, and you have seen the purpose of the Lord, how the Lord
is compassionate and merciful.

¹² But above all, my brothers, do not swear, either by heaven
or by earth or by any other oath, but let your "yes" be yes and
your "no" be no, so that you may not fall under condemnation.

The Prayer of Faith

¹³ Is anyone among you suffering? Let him pray. Is anyone
cheerful? Let him sing praise. ¹⁴ Is anyone among you sick? Let
him call for the elders of the church, and let them pray over
him, anointing him with oil in the name of the Lord. ¹⁵ And the
prayer of faith will save the one who is sick, and the Lord will
raise him up. And if he has committed sins, he will be forgiven.
¹⁶ Therefore, confess your sins to one another and pray for one
another, that you may be healed. The prayer of a righteous person has great power as it is working. ¹⁷ Elijah was a man with a
nature like ours, and he prayed fervently that it might not rain,
and for three years and six months it did not rain on the earth.
¹⁸ Then he prayed again, and heaven gave rain, and the earth
bore its fruit.

¹⁹ My brothers, if anyone among you wanders from the
truth and someone brings him back, ²⁰ let him know that whoever brings back a sinner from his wandering will save his soul
from death and will cover a multitude of sins.